# DOGS SET I

# DALMATIANS

Heidi Mathea
ABDO Publishing Company

# visit us at
# www.abdopublishing.com

Published by ABDO Publishing Company, 8000 West 78th Street, Edina, Minnesota 55439. Copyright © 2011 by Abdo Consulting Group, Inc. International copyrights reserved in all countries. No part of this book may be reproduced in any form without written permission from the publisher. The Checkerboard Library™ is a trademark and logo of ABDO Publishing Company.

Printed in the United States of America, North Mankato, Minnesota.
042010
092010

 PRINTED ON RECYCLED PAPER

Cover Photo: Peter Arnold
Interior Photos: Corbis pp. 7, 15, 17; Getty Images pp. 4, 20–21; iStockphoto pp. 9, 13; Peter Arnold pp. 10, 11; Photolibrary p. 19

Editor: Megan M. Gunderson
Art Direction & Cover Design: Neil Klinepier

## Library of Congress Cataloging-in-Publication Data

Mathea, Heidi, 1979-
 Dalmatians / Heidi Mathea.
    p. cm. --  (Dogs)
 Includes index.
 ISBN 978-1-61613-405-1
 1.  Dalmatian dog--Juvenile literature.  I. Title.
 SF429.D3M38 2011
 636.72--dc22

                               2010009938

# CONTENTS

# THE DOG FAMILY

Did you know all dogs are related to the gray wolf? More than 12,000 years ago, humans discovered wolves made good hunting partners.

Over time, people **domesticated** and **bred** these wild animals.  They became the dog breeds we know and love.  Today, there are more than 400 of them!  All these breeds belong to the family **Canidae**.

Dogs perform many jobs and fill various roles for humans.  Some are simply lapdogs, such as the pug.  They make excellent cuddle buddies.  Others are bred to be active.  This includes the Dalmatian.  It is the only spotted dog breed.

Humans bred this **unique**-looking animal to have **endurance**.  The energetic Dalmatian needs lots of exercise.  This beautiful animal makes an excellent pet for an active, fun-loving family.

*Dogs come in a variety of shapes and sizes.  Yet they are all related!*

# DALMATIANS

The Dalmatian is an old **breed**. Spotted dogs appear in paintings dating back to ancient Egyptian times! Because the Dalmatian goes back so far, historians are unsure where it began. However, experts believe these dogs are named for Dalmatia, Croatia.

Throughout history, Dalmatians have had a close relationship with horses. Dalmatians were used as coach dogs in England. They ran beside horse-drawn coaches. While traveling at night, the dogs guarded the carriages and the horses.

Dalmatians eventually moved into firehouses with horse-drawn fire wagons. Firefighters welcomed these useful dogs. When an alarm bell rang, Dalmatians led the fire wagons out of the station!

The **American Kennel Club** recognized the **breed** in 1888. Today, Dalmatians are still **mascots** for U.S. firehouses. Schoolchildren delight in seeing these furry, four-legged firefighters!

*Dalmatians have a long history with firefighters.*

# What They're Like

The Dalmatian **breed** is energetic and fun loving. Due to careful breeding, Dalmatians can run for hours without tiring. They especially enjoy playing and exercising with their owners.

Dalmatians are smart, even-tempered animals that love people. Like any family member, they need lots of love in return. These fiercely loyal dogs make fine family pets. They show affection for children and delight in watching over their families.

*Like all dogs, Dalmatians need loving owners who will offer them safe homes.*

# COAT AND COLOR

This puppy's spots are just starting to appear.

The spotted Dalmatian is easily recognized throughout the world. But, did you know Dalmatian puppies are born pure white? It's true! Their spots begin appearing at two weeks of age.

With its spotted coat, the Dalmatian looks different from any other dog breed.

The Dalmatian's lovely coat is short, **dense**, fine, and sleek. Black or brown spots dot the white base coat. The spots vary in size from dime sized to half-dollar sized.

# SIZE

The **unique**-looking Dalmatian is a long, lean dog. Its chest is deep, and its back is strong. Powerful legs support the muscular body. This beautiful creature has a long, graceful tail that curves up slightly. However, it should not curl over the dog's back.

Floppy ears sit high on the Dalmatian's head. The head should be in balance with the dog's body. The Dalmatian has medium-sized eyes that are brown or blue. This outgoing dog wears an alert, intelligent expression.

The adult Dalmatian measures between 19 and 23 inches (48 and 58 cm) tall. It weighs 50 to 55 pounds (23 to 25 kg).

**The Dalmatian is a
graceful-looking creature.**

# CARE

Dalmatians are a good fit for many families. They live to please their owners. However, they can become naughty if they are not exercised. It is important to have a large, fenced-in yard for these runners.

Dalmatians **shed** a lot! Their short coats need regular brushing. This will help prevent their hair from covering your furniture. Dalmatians also need their nails clipped and their ears cleaned.

Good health doesn't stop at grooming. A veterinarian can help keep a Dalmatian in top form. He or she can provide **vaccines**. In addition, the veterinarian can **spay** or **neuter** puppies at six months old.

The veterinarian you choose should have experience with the Dalmatian breed.

# FEEDING

To keep their energy up, Dalmatians need a well-balanced diet. A high-quality commercial food will help keep these active dogs healthy.

A small puppy needs at least four meals a day. By six months, owners can reduce feedings to twice a day. Once the dog stops growing, a single daily feeding should be enough.

In addition to healthy food, a Dalmatian needs lots of fresh water. A water bowl should sit next to the dog's food dish. Many owners prefer sturdy plastic or stainless steel bowls.

Dalmatians must be exercised every day so they do not gain weight. An overweight Dalmatian is not a healthy dog. Being active together will keep you and your pet happy and healthy!

**Don't let a Dalmatian's sweet face fool you into feeding it table scraps!**

# THINGS THEY NEED

A Dalmatian should live indoors. It is a social animal that needs to be with its family as much as possible.

When it is time to rest, your Dalmatian needs its own space. A crate provides the dog with a quiet place to sleep. A blanket makes the crate warm and comfortable. Another popular choice for a new puppy is a soft dog bed.

While your dog is awake, toys are a must. They will keep it from chewing your stuff. Puppies especially love to chew. So, hide your shoes! Without a toy handy, they'll grab the nearest object.

An owner should have a leash available for walks. Also, your four-legged friend needs an identification tag attached to its collar. The tag helps people track you down if your dog becomes lost.

*Toys are a great way to exercise a Dalmatian's body and brain.*

# PUPPIES

Female Dalmatians who are **pregnant** carry their young for about nine weeks. Puppies are born tiny and helpless. Their mothers feed and care for them. After about two weeks, the puppies can see and hear.

Dalmatian puppies can go to new, loving families after eight to ten weeks. Is a Dalmatian the right fit for you? If so, look for a reliable **breeder** or a rescue organization.

Slowly start introducing your Dalmatian puppy to new people, animals, and surroundings. This will make it less fearful of new things.

Begin training your dog the same day you bring it home. Dalmatians are more easily trained when they are young. And, training helps them grow into sweet, mature dogs. With proper care, Dalmatians can be loving family members for about 11 to 13 years.

**Dalmatian puppies are curious explorers.**

# GLOSSARY

**American Kennel Club** - an organization that studies and promotes interest in purebred dogs.

**breed** - a group of animals sharing the same ancestors and appearance. A breeder is a person who raises animals. Raising animals is often called breeding them.

**Canidae** (KAN-uh-dee) - the scientific Latin name for the dog family. Members of this family are called canids. They include domestic dogs, wolves, jackals, foxes, and coyotes.

**dense** - thick or compact.

**domesticate** - to adapt an animal to life with humans.

**endurance** - the ability to sustain a long, stressful effort or activity.

**mascot** - a person, an animal, or an object adopted by a group as a symbol or for good luck.

**neuter** (NOO-tuhr) - to remove a male animal's reproductive organs.

**pregnant** - having one or more babies growing within the body.

**shed** - to cast off hair, feathers, skin, or other coverings or parts by a natural process.

**spay** - to remove a female animal's reproductive organs.

**unique** - being the only one of its kind.

**vaccine** (vak-SEEN) - a shot given to prevent illness or disease.

# WEB SITES

To learn more about Dalmatians, visit ABDO Publishing Company on the World Wide Web at **www.abdopublishing.com**. Web sites about Dalmatians are featured on our Book Links page. These links are routinely monitored and updated to provide the most current information available.

# INDEX